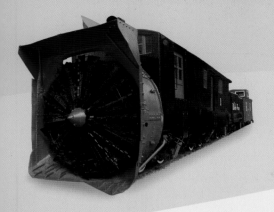

This Book Belongs to...

....

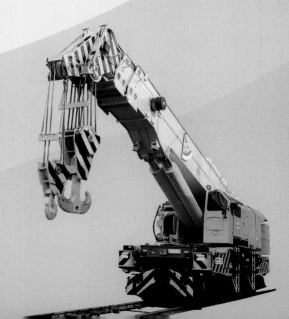

LONDON, NEW YORK,
MELBOURNE, MUNICH, AND DELHI

Editor Charlie Gardner
Designer Fiona Gowen
Producton Editor Vivianne Ridgeway
Production Controller Louise Kelly

First published in the United States in 2009
by DK Publishing
375 Hudson Street
New York, New York 10014

10 11 12 13 10 9 8 7 6
SD422—03/09

DK books are available at special discounts when purchased in bulk for
sales promotions, premiums, fundraising, or educational use. For details, contact:
DK Publishing Special markets
375 Hudson Street
New York, New York 10014
specialSales@dk.com

A catalog record for this book is
available from the Library of Congress.

ISBN: 978-0-7566-4552-6

Printed and bound in China by L-Rex

Discover more at
www.dk.com

The publisher would like to thank the following for
their kind permission to reproduce their photographs:

(Key: a-above; b-below/bottom; c-center; f-far; l-left; r-right; t-top)

Alamy Images: Martin Plöb/INSADCO Photography 11br. Alvey and Towers: 8-9, 10-11, 12-13, 15tr, 20bl,
crb, 20-21b, 21cl. Corbis: Richard Ross 14cra; Siracusa Productions, Inc./Transtock 14bc;
Joseph Sohm/Visions of America br (sticker sheet), 15bl. Cowans Sheldon: 3br, 18, 19, 21br, 22cr.
DK Images: FSTOP Pte. Ltd., Singapore cra (sticker sheet); Museum of Transportation, St Louis, MO ca (sticker sheet);
National Railway Museum, York 6cl. iStockphoto.com: Chad McDermott tl (sticker sheet), 15cla;
Niknikon 15crb. Raymond Lewis: 17tr. Jacket images: Front: Alvey and Towers.

All other images © Dorling Kindersley

For further information see: www.dkimages.com

See how they go!

Train

Smokin' steam train!

I AM A STEAM LOCOMOTIVE

SEE HOW I GO!

1155 S·H 2·18

COAL WAGON

My big wheels are turned by pistons powered by steam. A coal fire heats water in my boiler to make the steam.

Smoke from my fire comes out of the smokestack at the front of my boiler.

Behind me is my tender where I store lots of coal and water to keep my fire burning and my wheels turning.

SMOKESTACK

BOILER

TENDER

Locomotives like me ran on the very first railroads in the United States, more than 100 years ago.

Marvelous monorail!

I AM A MONORAIL TRAIN

SEE HOW I GO!

I run on just one special rail—a monorail.

DRIVER'S CAB

MONORAIL

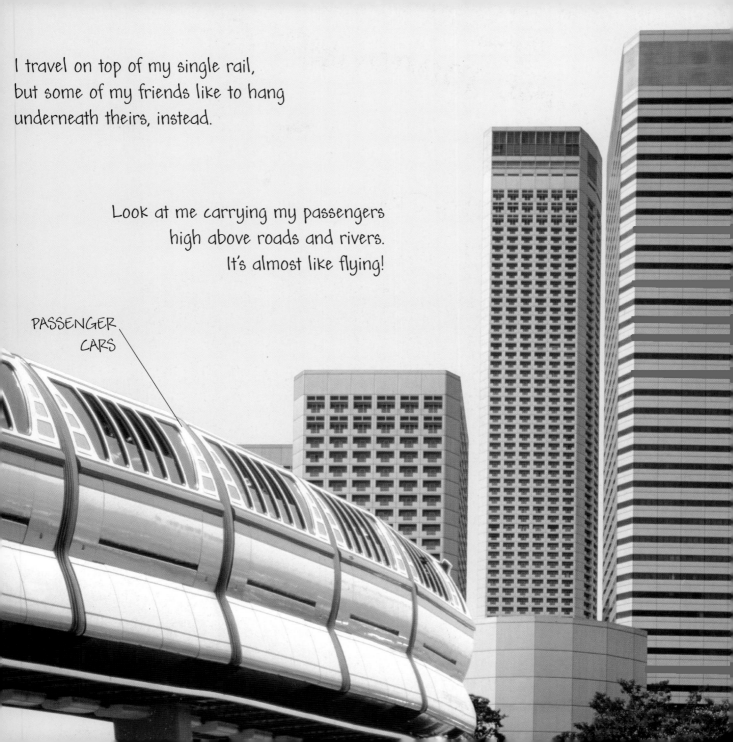

I travel on top of my single rail,
but some of my friends like to hang
underneath theirs, instead.

Look at me carrying my passengers
high above roads and rivers.
It's almost like flying!

PASSENGER
CARS

Magical mountain train!

I AM A MOUNTAIN TRAIN

SEE HOW I GO!

I'm a special kind of tram car that can carry passengers up hills and mountains.

STEP

Look how I climb steep hills without slipping. It's like magic! How do I do it?

PANTOGRAPH (ELECTRIC PICK-UP)

With my extra wheel—a powered cog wheel with gripping teeth.

My cog wheel grips an extra rail. It's the track in the middle that looks like a zipper.

EXTRA RAIL

Electric express!

I AM A HIGH-SPEED
EXPRESS TRAIN

SEE HOW I GO!

WIPER BLADES

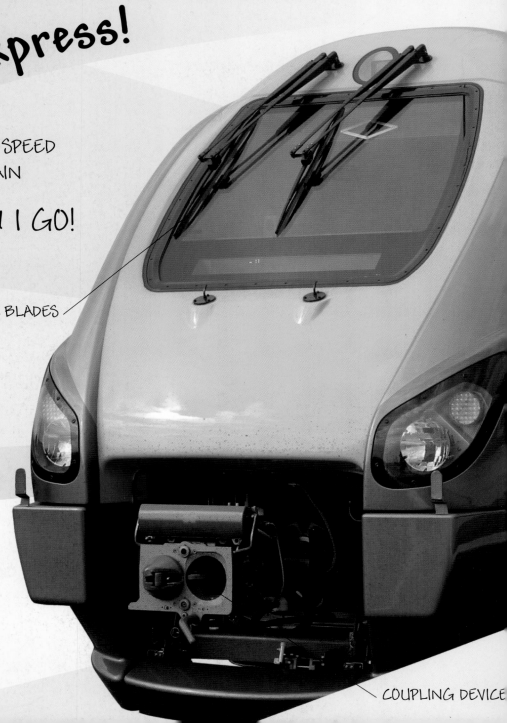

I am smooth, streamlined, and I can go fast! Watch me race at 180 miles per hour. That's three times faster than the cars on the highway!

COUPLING DEVICE

POWER LINES

My mega motors run on electricity that I pick up from the power lines above me.

CONDUCTOR

SLIDING DOORS

My rail tracks are extra-strong and straight, so I can go fast for most of my journey.

Fantastic freight train!

I AM A FREIGHT TRAIN

SEE HOW I GO!

BOXCAR

So many things are transported in freight cars: gravel, coal, gas, lumber, steel, machinery, tractors, wheat. . .

. . .construction materials, automobiles, trucks, military vehicles, frozen food, and cargo containers.

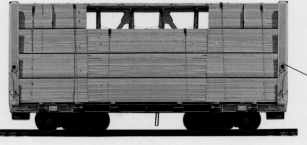

LUMBER CAR

GAS TANK CAR

RPBX 23123
LD LMT 204400 LB 92 700 KG
LT WT 56800 LB 26 800 KG

GRAVEL CAR

Look at me pulling these freight cars through the desert. This train is over a mile a long.

COAL CAR

CABOOSE

At the back of the train is the caboose where my conductor lives. From the top window, you can see all the cars and the locomotive.

Super snow train!

I AM A SNOW TRAIN

SEE HOW I GO!

When the snow on the tracks is too deep for even a snowplow, that's when I come to the rescue.

On the front of my train is a snow blower.

It's like a giant fan with propeller blades that cut through the snow and blow it away to the side of the tracks.

The locomotive behind me pushes me slowly forward. At top speed I can clear over 40 yards of deep snow in a minute.

Big railroad crane!

I AM A BIG RAILROAD CRANE

SEE HOW I GO!

BOOM

NEW TRACK

I am just like a crane you might see on a construction site, only I can run on rails.

You'll see me whenever there is construction to be done on the railroad.

My powerful boom is great for lifting heavy rail tracks and ties, or sections of bridges or buildings.

WINCH

DRIVER'S CAB

I'm so strong, I can lift things that weigh as much as 100 automobiles!

See how they go!

STEAM TRAIN

MOUNTAIN
RAILWAY TRAIN

MONORAIL TRAIN

SNOW TRAIN

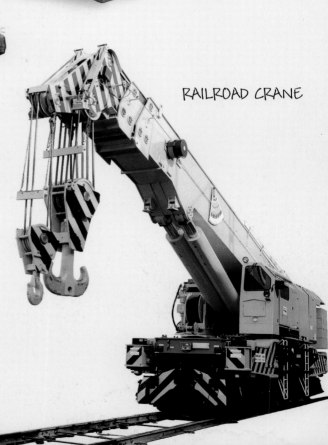

HIGH-SPEED TRAIN

RAILROAD CRANE

FREIGHT TRAIN

See How They GO!

Other titles:

Fire Truck
ISBN 978-0-7566-4553-3

Trucks
ISBN 978-0-7566-5168-8

Diggers
ISBN 978-0-7566-5167-1

Cars
ISBN 978-0-7566-5231-9

Emergency Vehicles
ISBN 978-07566-5230-2